THE HIGHEST PRIORITY IN LIFE

KNOWING GOD

D1177118

THE HIGHEST PRIORITY IN LIFE

KNOWING GOD

BOB HOEKSTRA

COSTA MESA, CA

KNOWING GOD

Copyright © 2016 Living in Christ Ministries
International Prison Ministry
Printed in 2016

Library of Congress Control Number: 2016930042
ISBN: 978-0-9772886-6-3

PUBLISHED AND DISTRIBUTED BY

International Prison Ministry / IPM Books
Living in Christ Ministries
PO Box 2868
Costa Mesa, CA 92628-2868

Edited by Heidi Ceballos,
(Daughter of Bob Hoekstra)
Book cover and interior layout by Living in Christ Ministries
Printed in the United States of America

DEDICATION

This book is dedicated first and foremost to our wonderful Lord. It is also dedicated to its author who served the Lord faithfully during his pilgrimage here on the earth.

May many lives be touched and encouraged by the truths contained in these pages, and may it be our heart's desire to get to know the Lord in a deeper way. May knowing the Lord become our highest priority in life.

PASTOR BOB HOEKSTRA

Pointing people
to the Lord
and to His Word

ABOUT THE AUTHOR

Bob Hoekstra was the Founder and Director of Living in Christ Ministries (LICM) until he went home to be with the Lord in 2011. He and his wife, Dini, were married for over 45 years and have three children. Bob graduated from Dallas Theological Seminary with a Masters In Theology Degree.

Bob was an insightful author and teacher, whom the Lord used greatly to share the Word of God with the body of Christ. His 45 years of ministry included pastoring two churches. He also taught at many conferences, retreats, and Bible college campuses across America and around the world.

Bob Hoekstra's Bible teachings can still be heard in a variety of media resources (CD, DVD, MP3, BD), on radio stations across America, and on OnePlace.com.

ABOUT LICM

Living in Christ Ministries is a ministry dedicated to pointing God's people to the Lord and to His Word. We are a ministry that "Proclaims Christ to Christians."

In order to grow in maturity, in wholeness, in fruitfulness, and in Christ-likeness, we must be feeding on the truth from God's Word about the Lord Jesus Christ, who lives in us as our hope of glory (Colossians 1:27-28).

We invite you to visit our website to learn more about God's Word and His all sufficient grace. God's desire is for His people to get to know Him better day by day. May it be our heart's desire to grow in the grace and knowledge of our Lord and Savior Jesus Christ (2 Peter 3:18).

LIVING IN CHRIST MINISTRIES
PO BOX 2848 COSTA MESA, CA 92628
LIVINGINCHRIST.ORG

TABLE OF CONTENTS

"That I may know Him and the power of His resurrection, and the fellowship of His sufferings, being conformed to His death."
- Philippians 3:10

KNOWING GOD

If one were to ask you the question, "What is the number one priority in your life," what would you answer? Your response to such a question is of primary importance because it reveals what motivates you, what absorbs your thoughts, what sustains you, and that for which you are willing to sacrifice all else.

God is very much interested in what takes first place in our lives, and in

1

many ways and throughout the Scriptures, He lets us know what must be in that place. The highest priority in life, He declares, is growing in our knowledge and relationship with the Lord. There is nothing higher than knowing the Lord, growing in friendship with the Lord, and developing a growing personal relationship with Jesus Christ. The Apostle Paul affirms this truth:

> *"But what things were gain to me, these I have counted loss for Christ. Yet indeed I also count all things loss for the excellence of the knowledge of Christ Jesus my Lord..." (Philippians 3:7, 8).*

"Excellence" speaks of something that stands out, rises above, is superior in rank, and is translated at times in the New Testament as "higher" or "supreme." Another way to state this is the surpassing value of knowing the Lord. Knowing the Lord is what life is all about. Having an ongoing, growing relationship with Jesus is to be life's ultimate reality, life's highest purpose, the highest priority in life, and our reason for living. Knowing Jesus Christ is the very definition of eternal life according to John:

> *"And this is eternal life, that they may know You, the only true God, and Jesus Christ whom You have sent" (John 17:3).*

The Apostle Paul concludes that everything else is loss when contrasted with knowing the Lord. There is nothing left if we don't know the Lord, and those who forsake the path of getting to know the Lord are forsaking God forever. David, seeing the importance of this, counseled his son Solomon to get to know the Lord God.

> *"As for you, my son Solomon, know the God of your father, and serve Him with a loyal heart and with a willing mind; for the LORD searches all hearts and understands all the intent of the thoughts. If you seek Him, He will be found by you; but if you forsake Him, He will cast you off forever"* (1 Chronicles 28:9).

Men boast in their wisdom, thinking they know how to put life together better than anyone else. They take pride in their appearances, their status, their influence, their riches. God warns against such boasting, however, giving us instead something in which we ought to glory.

> *"Thus says the LORD: 'Let not the wise man glory in his wisdom. Let not the mighty man glory in his might. Nor let the rich man glory in his riches; But let him who glories glory in this, That he understands and knows Me, That I am the LORD, exercising lovingkindness, judgment, and righteousness in the earth. For in these I delight,' says the LORD" (Jeremiah 9:23, 24).*

If we want something to boast about, we should glory in this, that we understand and know the Lord.

In this country, there can be some serious boasting by many sports fans for their favorite teams. It can become a virtual religion to some, where they gather together to watch their idols, raise their arms, dance in the aisles and shout. Praise be to our team! Boasting, going berserk for something so insignificant, so transient. Followers of the Lord Jesus, who should be the real fanatics on planet earth, often consider so lightly the awesome privilege of knowing our excellent Savior for time and eternity. Boasting in the Lord Jesus is a true demonstration of the reality that we know Him. We could only understate His greatness and His glory.

"But let him who glories glory in this, That he understands and knows Me, That I am the LORD..." (Jeremiah 9:24).

KNOWING HIM WHO IS TRUE

Though we can never fully know God because His mind is so much higher than ours, He does reveal Himself little by little to those who seek Him.

"And you will seek Me and find Me, when you search for Me with all your heart" (Jeremiah 29:13).

Even understanding Him a little is the most excellent treasure of life.

Knowing that He exercises loving-kindness, judgment, and righteousness in the earth, and that He has a loyal steadfast love for His people every day, every night, every hour, every moment! To know that the Lord is committed to us with an everlasting lovingkindness is more than all the riches of this life. Consider that He exercises judgment in the world, that He alone decides what is to happen, that He will take care of things. We can know and rest in that. Even though it looks as though there is no justice or good judgment anywhere, God is not through yet. His judgment is righteous and He will judge the world righteously.

> *"He shall judge the world in righteousness, And He shall administer judgment for the people in uprightness" (Psalm 9:8).*

Knowing the Lord is what everlasting life is all about. Those who reject the knowledge of the Lord are dead while they yet live, and after physical death, will exist in that deadness forever. We who know Him, however, have eternal life now and will live with Him forever.

Before God shined the knowledge of the Lord into our hearts, we as others, had darkened hearts. We walked in darkness, fulfilling our natural wicked desires.

> *"For it is the God who commanded light to shine out of darkness, who has shone in our hearts to give the light of the knowledge of the glory of God in the face of Jesus Christ" (2 Corinthians 4:6).*

Do you remember how dark your heart was before the light of God was shining in there? Think of Carlsbad Caverns with the lights out. So, too, were our hearts dark with sin, being selfish, unreliable, dishonest, deceitful, self-centered, motivated to chase everything God said to leave alone, and to leave alone everything after which God said to chase.

But the day came when the light of the knowledge of the glory of God, in the face of Christ, began to shine in our hearts. Didn't that change everything? We came out of darkness into His marvelous light. It was all in the face of Jesus Christ, shining the light of the knowledge of the glory of God.

"...I am the light of the world. He who follows Me shall not

walk in darkness, but have the light of life" (John 8:12).

I grew up in a pastor's home, and by the time I was out of high school my parents were tired of dragging me to church, so I wasn't going. The pastor talked about God. What a bore; what a drag, how irrelevant. I wanted some action. And from the ages of fifteen to twenty-five, I went deep into the world, messing up my life and messing up the lives of others. After ten years, God finally got through to me, the Word impacting me most strongly through the one who was to become my wife. The light was beginning to dawn on me as I realized that everything I had been living for was a lie. I was crushed and defeated. I saw that Jesus Christ was the one I should have been pursuing, discovering that God loves a broken spirit

11

and a contrite heart. So I wept and He forgave. I confessed and He gave new life. The light started to shine in, and I saw it was the face of Jesus Christ.

"And we know that the Son of God has come and has given us an understanding, that we may know Him who is true; and we are in Him who is true, in His Son Jesus Christ. This is the true God and eternal life" (1 John 5:20).

This is such a beautiful verse. It is all about knowing our wonderful Lord.

We did not know the truth before we came to Jesus. We lived a lie, always afraid that people would find out what phonies we were. God then exposed our lies, gave us the truth, and we no longer had to pretend anymore. It is just so freeing not to have to put on a show. It is so liberating to know that the Lord can change our hearts and set us on the right path, a path of righteousness and truth. It is wonderful to let go of our past and all the things that used to take higher priority in our lives other than knowing the Lord.

Oh, the excellence of the knowledge of the Lord! It is life's greatest treasure, and is why Paul said he counted all things loss and rubbish in comparison to gaining Christ and knowing Him better:

> "Yet indeed I also count all things loss for the excellence of the knowledge of Christ Jesus my Lord, for whom I have suffered the loss of all things, and

count them as rubbish, that I may gain Christ" (Philippians 3:8).

Paul considered everything but the knowledge of the Lord as loss, rubbish, more literally, dung. If anything competes with, or gets in the way of, knowing God, Paul said: I count it loss. I count it as a pile of manure and don't want anything to do with it. May we all have that perspective!

HINDRANCES TO GETTING TO KNOW HIM

So many things that look so important can get in the way of our knowing the Lord. For many, it is often even the good things that get in the way, subtle hindrances that are not readily identified as rubbish. It could be a job, for example. Even though a man must work, he shouldn't worship the job or live for it. The reason he has to work is because God said to work, so working is right. God has ordained it, and there is value in it.

"That you may have a walk worthy of the Lord, fully pleasing Him, being fruitful in every good work and increasing in the knowledge of God...and to work with your own hands..." (Colossians 1:10; 1 Thessalonians 4:11).

We do not as the world, work to get, however, because we have been promised by God that He will supply all of our needs according to His riches in Christ Jesus (Philippians 4:19). So we work to obey, and God uses us on the job. More often, perhaps, He uses the job on us. But He does not want our work or our job getting in the way of knowing Him. We can end up being slaves to a job instead of being bondslaves to Christ. If we commit to knowing Him, not to living for our job, He will put our job in the right place, with the right perspective. He might even give us a new job, since our boss might not like having someone around that lives for God rather than for himself.

Sometimes the opinions of others can get in the way of our knowing God. We might be tempted to think, "I'd better not get too fanatical. They're going to think I'm strange, a Jesus freak." So we lay off a little, we tone it down some concerning the Lord when others are around, since we think their opinions matter, after all. There we are, jumping back into the dung heap! Knowing and pursuing God might very well result in our having lousy reputations with those who have no interest in Him, but conversely, great reputations with those who do. We become a good testimony of the Lord Jesus. It actually sorts out quite beautifully.

We may have habits that hinder our growth in Jesus Christ. Though perhaps there is nothing inherently wrong with a particular practice, if it is getting in the way of really knowing the Lord, it is to effectively jump back into the dung heap. We ought to ask the Lord to give us the understanding and openness to discern those things that are getting in the way of our knowing Him, and be willing to see them as dung. That should motivate us to leave them alone.

Hobbies can be another deterrent to knowing God. Although they are used of God for blessing, refreshment, and sometimes even an avenue of witnessing, they can also become a monstrous dung heap, interfering with our growth in the Lord. Hobbies can so captivate our minds that we are driven to indulge ourselves in them. That is to dive back into the dung heap! We need to be willing to count anything that doesn't contribute to the growth of our relationship with the Lord as loss.

Another subtle way we can be hindered in knowing the Lord is through busy religious activity. As believers, we can easily become busy and distracted in our serving and forget what the highest priority in life is all about. In Luke chapter 10 we can learn from the example of Mary and Martha how we can be deterred from focusing to knowing the Lord by being buried in much service for the Lord.

"...He (Jesus) entered a certain village; and a certain woman named Martha welcomed Him into her house. And she had a

sister called Mary, who also sat at Jesus' feet and heard His word. But Martha was distracted with much serving, and she approached Him and said, Lord do You not care that my sister has left me to serve alone? Therefore tell her to help me. And Jesus answered and said to her. 'Martha, Martha, you are worried and troubled about many things. But one thing is needed, and Mary has chosen that good part, which will not be taken away from her' " (Luke 10:38-42).

Many hindrances can keep us from knowing the Lord and making Him our highest priority in life. Only at His feet can we find true life.

FINDING
LIFE

I f the number one priority of knowing the Lord is out of order, everything else in our lives will be out of order. If this priority is in order, everything else will be growing into its proper perspective and its proper place. As we grow in knowing the Lord, we can allow Him to fit these other things in any time, any place, or any way He wants, if He wants. Only then are we able to gain Christ, as Paul points out at the end of Philippians 3:8:

> " ...and count them as rubbish,
> that I may gain Christ."

Allowing Jesus Christ to more extensively work in and through our lives by experiencing Him more and more is what it is to gain Christ.

> "...that I may gain Christ and
> be found in Him..." (Philippians
> 3:8, 9).

There is only one of two places in the universe any individual person can be found, and that is in Christ or out of Christ. We are either in Christ, in the new life He gives, or in Adam, in that natural life passed on to us through our parents. If we are in Christ, we have His righteousness; if we are in Adam, we have only self-righteousness, derived from the Law.

It is the fundamental matter of righteousness that is at issue here. If we are going to know a holy and pure God, we cannot come to Him and say, "Here I am. I want to meet you." Because of our sin and guilt, we can't even approach Him. Filthy rags is God's description of our righteousness.

"But we are all like an unclean thing, And all our righteousnesses are like filthy rags..." (Isaiah 64:6).

So how do we get close to God? The answer is found in Jesus Christ. He came from the Father to reveal Himself to us and then to offer Himself up as a sacrifice for us. He came to say:

"Come to Me...I am the Way, the Truth, and the Life. No one

comes to the Father except through Me" (Matthew 11:28; John 14:6).

If you want to know the Father, I am the Way. If you want to know what He is like, I will show Him to you. I and the Father are one. We are the same: same righteousness, same holiness, same love, same ability to forgive (John 5:19-22; 14:6,7).

Those of us who repent of our sins are cleansed, forgiven, and placed in Jesus Christ. His righteousness becomes our righteousness. We are then able to come before the Father in the name of Jesus, and pray:

Father, in Jesus' name, forgive me a sinner; Father, in Jesus' name, have mercy on me and

*hear me; Father, in Jesus' name,
work in my life.*

Our relationship with the Father is
based on the righteousness of Jesus
Christ, and we are asking God to work
in our lives according to what Jesus
would deserve, to treat us as He de-
serves to be treated. That is a good
place to be, isn't it? It is exactly where
we are if we are found in Christ.

*"And be found in Him, not hav-
ing my own righteous-
ness..." (Philippians 3:9).*

We don't establish a relationship
with God on our own best effort, because that would come from the Law.
The Law merely showed us the stan-
dard, which was revealed by His com-
mandments. The Law was never in-

tended to be the means by which we come to know God, because all have sinned and come short of the glory of God (Romans 3:23). And the wages of sin is death (Romans 6:23).

What we need is the righteousness of One who measured up to the righteous, holy, glorious Law of God, and that One is Jesus Christ. If we believe in Jesus, He becomes our Lord and Savior, the Father finds us in Him, and the righteousness of Christ is now ours by faith in Christ. When we are held up to the Law of God, we measure up in Christ, enabling us to have a relationship with the Father.

If you have never put your faith in the Lord Jesus Christ, you must stand before the God who wants to be your loving Father, but as Judge, will have to condemn you on the basis of your righteousness. It simply does not measure up. Though that may sound like bad news, it is good news to know where you stand.

You need the righteousness that comes only from God by faith, and you can only receive it by believing on the Lord Jesus Christ. If you have never done so, even now in your heart, call upon His name:

> *Yes, Lord, I am guilty. I am a sinner. I do not measure up. I cannot have a relationship with You on my own, but I understand there is one available through Jesus Christ. Lord, I repent; I admit I need that kind of cleansing and forgiveness. By faith I ask You to forgive me.*

Clothe me with the righteousness in Your Son. Be my Lord and Savior. Amen.

If you have received Christ as Lord and Savior, then take Him at His Word.

"That if you confess with your mouth the Lord Jesus and believe in your heart that God has raised Him from the dead, you will be saved. For with the heart one believes unto righteousness, and with the mouth confession is made unto salvation" (Romans 10:9, 10).

By faith you will have what He offers, because He keeps His word. But do it today, that you, too, may be found in His righteousness.

THREE WAYS OF GETTING TO KNOW HIM

O nce we are found in His right-eousness, we can develop a relationship with God through Jesus Christ, the Son of God. The Lord wants to stir in us a passion to grow in knowing Him. In this passage, God re-veals three ways in which He wants us to be getting to know Him:

"That I may know Him and the power of His resurrection, and the fellowship of His sufferings,

being conformed to His death" (Philippians 3:10).

If someone were to ask us, What is our highest priority in life? We can bring it down to just one succinct phrase: *"That I may know Him."* If they ask, what are you all about? What's your life all about? Where are you headed? What are you after? We can answer: *"That I may know Him."* If they ask how they can pray for us, we can answer: *"That I may know Him."* What do you think life's all about? *"That I may know Him."* It is an astounding phrase; it just explains so much.

When we meet someone and get acquainted with them, we go through things together. We communicate together. We face things together. We get to know each other. It works the same way with God.

"That I may know Him and the power of His resurrection..." (Philippians 3:10).

Of the three ways of getting to know God, this is almost unanimously everyone's preference. If you think about it, how would you rather get to know Him: in the power of His resurrection, in the fellowship of His sufferings, or being conformable to His death? Most would answer that they would prefer knowing Him through the power of His resurrection. But the choice is not ours. He chooses the way in which He will reveal Himself to us.

Getting to know the Lord through the power of His resurrection is our initial acquaintanceship with Him. We come to the Lord dead in trespasses and sins (Ephesians 2:1)—broken, guilty, and alienated, with no life in us at all. That is how we are first introduced to Jesus Christ. In Him we find life and are raised to newness of life. We get a taste of the power of the resurrection.

In the 6th chapter of Romans, Paul speaks of the power of the resurrection at work in us when he declares that we who believe in Him, died with Christ on the cross. We were buried with Him, and are raised with Him to newness of life.

I remember so vividly that process at work in my own life when I came to the Lord. It was the last week of 1965, and I was weeping heavily in my heart, thinking it was all over. I was dying. I was done. There was no way out. Except for His resurrection power, a reality of which I was not yet aware, this was true of my condition. Then I discovered that in calling on the name of the Lord, I was raised to newness of life. Oh, what a tremendous start to 1966! I was walking on resurrection ground! Everything looked different. Everything felt different. Everything was becoming different in my life. My perspective changed completely. That was resurrection hope.

When we come out of the deadness of sin and guilt, we are resurrected to new life, thus beginning a honeymoon, as it were, with our bridegroom. It is glorious. It is joy and laughter and delight and freedom. And, Oh! That thousand pound, hundred-thousand pound, million pound load of guilt—where did it go? I can walk rightly! The power of the resurrection. It is glorious!

We begin to know the Lord in that phase of our walk with Him. He is the God of resurrection, victorious over sin and death. But the Christian life is not going to be on resurrection ground all the time, contrary to the impression some give. The reality of life is that a bit down the trail—for some, a month; for some, a year; but sooner or later—it seems as though the resurrection fades, and a strange thing comes around called suffering.

Our initial response is to question our salvation, to question if God loves us, to wonder if He has forsaken us. What is happening is that He wants us to get more deeply acquainted with

Him. There is more to Jesus Christ than the power of the resurrection; there is also the fellowship of His sufferings.

When Jesus Christ was on the earth, He suffered greatly. He was a man of sorrows, acquainted with grief. He was persecuted and rejected. He was lied about, betrayed, forsaken, beaten, executed. And all of this was part of His serving the Father and reaching out to man.

As we get to know Him and start to walk His path, wanting to live in a way that is pleasing to Him, not everybody we meet is going to applaud us for being on resurrection ground. No, before we know it, someone will say, "Will you stop all that religious nonsense? You irritate me." Or the boss might say, "I thought that religious thing would kind of cool down, but let me tell you, if it doesn't, your out of here." Or a dear relative you know says, "That Jesus thing you got into is okay, but it's getting obnoxious. You used to be fun; now you're nothing but a drag." The good friend that would do just about anything to spend time with you now does everything to avoid you. What is happening is that the Lord wants us to see there is more to Him than resurrection power, and if we are going to know Him, He wants us to taste some of the suffering He endured on the earth.

We begin to suffer as He did by walking righteously with the Father. We receive some persecution, some rejection, beginning to learn the cost of obedience. It is not pleasant, but we do come to appreciate the Lord Jesus

Christ all the more. That is getting acquainted with the Lord through the fellowship of His sufferings.

We may come to a place where we accept a measure of suffering. But it can get worse, because there is also the process of being conformed to His death. This surely is the least chosen path, if the option were ever given. Some might venture out in faith, going deeper than having only a resurrected acquaintanceship with Him, recognizing that they need to be broken, weakened, rejected. But few choose to go further. What we come to discover, though, is that we don't have to choose it. It will come to us. Jesus shrank, as it were, from the cross, because of His holiness and His eternality. He was going to taste sin and death, and every part of His being shuddered at the cup of our sin and death. He didn't run to the cross, as it meant death and separation from the Father. He bled as He agonized over that cup as He cried out to the Father. But, He said:

> *"...nevertheless not My will, but Yours, be done" (Luke 22:42).*

The cross comes to us. Some try to run and hide from it, getting much assistance, unfortunately, from the church. Seminars are held in which we are, in effect, instructed to detour the cross of discipleship. We are told how to feel good about ourselves, how to believe in ourselves, how to be positive. In essence we are saying, "Nevertheless, not your will, but mine be done." But for those who really want to know the Father, who are committed to His will, there will be a conforming to His death.

It is the necessary response to the heart that cries out, "That I may know Him!"

What is being conformed to His death in practical terms? It involves experiencing impossible situations as we obey the Father. Sometimes it involves excruciating agony. In fact, the central, root word of excruciating is "crux": the cross, crucifixion. Being conformed to His death is often a matter of saying, "Not my will, but Yours be done," when we have pain that feels like death.

Conforming to His death also relates to those times in our Christian lives when only the faithfulness of the Father will deliver us. Maybe we have Jacob'd our way as far as we can go. Remember Jacob? His name means "schemer." There is a little bit of Jacob in all of us, isn't there? Sometimes the Lord allows a Jacob to get in the corner until he gets his hip out of joint. He has to limp and depend on the provision of God alone. Those are the times when he learns that there is no way out except through the Father's faithfulness, and that is being conformed to His death.

When Jesus cried out, *"...My God, My God, why have You forsaken Me" (Mark 15:34),* it is not that He did not know the ultimate answer. He was quoting out of Psalm 22, which was the answer. He knew the path that lay before Him. He was being made sin for all of us, and the only way out was the faithfulness of the Father:

"...Father, into Your hands I commit My spirit" (Luke 23:46).

Everything depended on the faithfulness of the Father at that moment.

We can get into places in which it becomes so clear to us that there is no way to go on or no way out, unless the faithful Father comes through. It could be persecution, financial impossibilities, relationship impossibilities, physical pain and suffering through health impossibilities, or the death of a loved one. Maybe you are there right now. This is being conformed to His death, which I like to call being entombed.

In my walk with the Lord these many years, I think I have been entombed about three times. I am not really looking for any more of those experiences, though I must say I got to know Him better each time. If there is another entombment, I don't want to shrink from it, because it is not pleasing to the Father to do so. It inhibits further growth in Him.

I can remember back in the 1970's thinking I was so dead. I had been a pastor for some years and there had been so many disappointments, so many discouragements, that I was finally crushed. It seemed as though all the life and faith and hope were drained out of me. I would lie around weeping at home, watching a church being traumatized through theological aberrations and things against which I had not yet learned how to contend. I was dying, being conformed to His death. The only way out was to be raised. Eventually, the Lord did raise me up. Perhaps this does not carry as much weight as Lazarus' being raised, but let me tell you, I have been raised three times. I remember being essentially as helpless as Lazarus, and He faithfully brought me out every single time.

Because we serve a God of resurrection, being conformed to His death is not a negative process, but a glorious opportunity to share again in His resurrected life. If it looks to you that it is all over, including your home, your job, and your Christian life; if the lies, the condemnation of the enemy, the attacks of even the brethren, are threatening to destroy you—remember, brothers and sisters, we serve a God of resurrection!

Do you know what happens when He calls us out of that tomb? We are back on resurrection ground! We are back tasting again the power of His resurrection. It is like a second honey-moon, and I remember even a third honeymoon. Oh, how could I forget? Once you have been raised, you are never the same. The enemy shouts, "I'll bury you!" Well, he just might. He has done it before, but the Lord will raise us, and that changes everything. We develop a new kind of faith, a resur-rection faith.

All that we have been discussing must be, to quote a great phrase out of Psalm 119, *"according to [His] word."* This subject of *"the power of His resur-rection, the fellowship of His suffer-ings, being conformed to His death,"* is not referring to some experiential pil-grimage we concoct to draw more closely to God. It is not that at all. Every bit of it, to be real, must be ac-cording to His Word, and His Word speaks much about all these things. So to validate all that we are going through, we must stay in the Word. We must keep hearing from God. Let Him speak to us about these things so we can avoid getting off on some tangent that will keep us from the very thing we thought we were pursuing.

Psalm 119 is all about God's Word and brings great encouragement and hope to our lives when we face impossibilities. Time and again the psalmist repeats, *"According to Your word"*:

> *"Revive me according to Your word...Strengthen me according to Your word...Be merciful to me according to Your word...Uphold me according to Your word...Give me understanding according to Your*

word... Deliver me according to Your word" (Psalm 119:25, 28, 58, 116, 169, 170).

Our life must conform to the Word of the Lord. The Lord wants us to be feeding daily upon His Word which will enable us to grow in knowing Him.

RESURRECTED LIVING

A s we are growing in knowing our resurrected Lord, He will work within us enabling us to live a resurrected life here on the earth, to which Paul alludes in these verses:

"That I may know Him (in all these ways)...If, by any means (if by anything God wants to take me through), I may attain to the resurrection from the dead" (Philippians 3:10-11).

Paul is not talking about the final resurrection of the just. He had already attained to that by being in Christ, by placing his faith in Christ. If you are in Christ, you have attained to the final resurrection in Christ as well. But we all should desire to attain to resurrected living, just as Paul desired to attain to such a life.

"If, by any means, I may attain to the resurrection from the dead" (Philippians 3:11).

What is this resurrection from the dead? The word here translated literally is, "out lifting," or "out resurrection." It is the only place in the Bible this term is found. It is a unique kind of resurrection, referring to being raised to a Christ-like, overcoming, victorious life in this dead world. This verse could be paraphrased something like this: "That I may be getting to know the Lord in such a life-transforming way, that more and more I respond in ways that lift me out, lift me up above this dead and dying world." Stated in an-other way, it is that I may live more and more like Jesus, my resurrected Lord.

As we go through life, we are not re-sponding to problems, situations, op-portunities, blessings, challenges, or decisions, as we did before we were saved or even as we did two, three, or five years ago when we knew the Lord at that level. As we grow in knowing the Lord, we can be raised to a higher and higher quality of life, and the more we get to know Him, the more we are able to live in a way that is resurrected, and "lifted up and out" from this dead world.

49

This world is dead. Much of the church world is dead! How do most Christians really live? Do they live above weak, fleshy, human thinking, deciding, and reacting? If they do not, let them get to know a resurrected Lord, and it will cause them to live an increasingly resurrected life. A dead world needs to see people who know a resurrected Lord and are living resurrected lives. So when the unconverted ask us why we do not react to difficulties and crises the way others do, we can respond that we have been raised out of that way of living. We can praise God that our resurrected Lord is working through us to express to others a noticeably resurrected life.

Resurrected living can come only from knowing a resurrected Lord. So let us be in the Word of God, that we may know Him, the Living Word. Let us pray as Paul did, in Ephesians 1:17:

> *"That the God of our Lord Jesus Christ, the Father of glory, may give to you (us) the spirit of wisdom and revelation in the knowledge of Him."*

Let us, like Paul, count all things loss for the excellence of the knowledge of Christ, and press on to know Him. Few, if any, knew the Lord better than the Apostle Paul in his day and age, when he wrote the following words:

> *"If, by any means, I may attain to the resurrection from the dead. Not that I have already attained, or am already perfected; but I press on, that I may lay hold of that for which Christ*

Jesus has also laid hold of me" (Philippians 3:11-12).

His humble confession that he had not yet reached maturity serves as a good reminder to us all of the importance of walking in humility, Jesus Christ Himself being *"meek and lowly" (Matthew 11:29).*

"If, by any means, I may attain…" (Philippians 3:11)

What is it that Paul had not already attained? He had not attained the full measure of resurrected living in a dead world. In other words, though Paul had been getting to know the Lord for twenty-five or thirty years, he confesses that he had not gotten to know the Lord so fully that in every way and every measure of living, he was living the resurrected life as the Lord lived. His life was not yet wholly an expression of resurrected living, and he desired to live above a dead world in which the resource for living is self, whose aim is self, whose striving is for self.

The more we know our resurrected Lord, the more we live on that resurrected plane. Paul's confession was that there was still some deadness to his life, some areas in which he still responded and thought and decided and prioritized as the dead world around him did. But, he said, *"I press on."*

And so should we press on! A brother told me once that he thought he had learned ninety or so percent of all the things he could learn about the Lord. So, he said, he was just waiting for glory. This was said to me fairly early on in my ministry, but it stayed with me. He was a godly man then and he is today, and I should have asked him when I spoke with him some time back if he had picked up the other ten percent yet. I would not be in the least surprised if he had changed his perspective on that.

We do not gain most of our understanding early on in our walk with the Lord and then just coast on, as it were, into glory. That does not fit this biblical picture at all. Paul says, he presses on, he moves forward in a purposeful, spiritual pilgrimage. Good synonyms for the phrase, "press on," are "to pursue" or "to follow after eagerly." It can also mean "endeavoring earnestly to acquire," or "reaching out to get hold of something." Jesus said, "*Come follow*

Me" (Matthew 19:21), and this fits so perfectly with knowing the Lord. Paul was pursuing eagerly after the Lord to know Him.

Paul, as a seasoned warrior in the battle, was not coasting. He was pressing on in order to lay hold of that for which Christ Jesus had also laid hold of him. Paul wanted to grasp something, to seize something. "Lay hold of" speaks of fully obtaining, taking possession of, fully entering into. That is what he was reaching out to do, to lay hold of, to seize that for which Christ Jesus had also laid hold of him.

When Paul (then Saul) was heading down the road to Damascus, he saw himself as God's great servant. He was on a mission to arrest the heretics who followed that itinerant Preacher who said, *"I am the way, the truth, and the life" (John 14:6).* Determined to purge Judaism of these infidels, he was an imposing figure at the time, with the backing and authority of the religious world. Then suddenly, without warning, the Lord laid hold of him in what may be considered classic, direct evangelism: "I want you!" Light from heaven blinded him, he fell off his mount, and this mighty man of valor in Judaism was brought to his knees. Basically, it was as if Jesus said to Paul:

"You did not choose Me, but I chose you..." (John 15:16).

That is the bottom line. No dead and blind man would choose God if He did not work by His Spirit to bring him toward Himself. The Lord just grabbed Paul, and it is a wonderful picture. Because the Lord laid hold of him, Paul wanted to lay hold of all the purposes God had for him. Paul also mentions this phrase "lay hold on" in the following verses pertaining to the beleiver laying hold on eternal life:

> *"Fight the good fight of faith, lay hold on eternal life, to which you were also called...storing up for themselves a good foundation for the time to come, that they may lay hold on eternal life" (1 Timothy 6:12, 19).*

The Apostle Paul wanted to grab all the fullness of life available to him in Christ. He pressed on to take another handful, as it were, by faith. The Lord had grabbed him for a reason, and now Paul wanted to grab all those purposes that the Lord had for him.

Jesus takes over our lives for a reason, and that is ultimately that we might get to know Him. How we make Him known is directly related to the depth to which we know Him, and as we are sent out into all the world to make disciples, our effectiveness is in direct proportion to how well we know Him. The more closely we follow him, the more confidently we can tell others the way. Discipleship is following the Lord; making disciples is helping people meet the Lord so they, too, can follow Him. May we press on to know the Lord, laying hold of His purposes for our life, allowing Him to conform us to His image along the way.

THE ONE NECESSARY THING

The Apostle Paul said that there was one thing he did, though there were actually so many things he did in his life. He was an apostle, a teacher, an evangelist, a disciple, a church planter, a writer, one who was involved in miracles, and the recipient of direct revelation and authority from the Lord. This man did and was so many things, and yet he says: *"one thing I do."* That a fully diversified walk with the Lord, touching all areas of life, can be summarized in such a way is an amazing insight into the kingdom of God and life in Christ.

> *"Brethren, I do not count myself to have apprehended (I haven't fully grasped all this yet); but one thing I do, forgetting those things which are behind and reaching forward to those things which are ahead" (Philippians 3:13).*

If one were to ask the Apostle Paul what he was doing in the ministry, he would say he was doing one thing. If you were to ask him when he was doing something that looked so different from a previous occasion, he could still say he was doing one thing. What is it that he did that covered so wide a front? He was pressing on to know the

Lord. It was that for which he was aiming, the surpassing excellence of knowing Christ Jesus the Lord.

What an amazing insight for us! That statement can summarize all our life in the Lord as we learn to live this way more and more. Jesus, in the Sermon on the Mount, said:

"...If therefore your eye is good, your whole body will be full of light" *(Matthew 6:22).*

This truth is echoed by these words of the Apostle Paul. If the eye which receives light is focused on the light source, the whole body is filled with that light. What if your eye is somewhere else, with maybe just a little cross beam of light coming in? That is so often the reality with us. Often, we are caught up in something else and we tend to hone in on that instead of the Lord Himself. But everything flows out from Him. All we need is found in Him. If the eye is single, the whole body is full of light, which is another way of saying, "one thing I do."

David was another man of many assignments and accomplishments, and yet he also said that he desired just one thing of the Lord. He wanted to dwell and be in God's house all the days of his life,

> *"One thing I have desired of the LORD, That will I seek: That I may dwell in the house of the LORD, All the days of my life, To behold the beauty of the LORD, And to inquire in His temple" (Psalm 27:4).*

David wanted to inquire of the Lord, and to behold His beauty. That is why this man had a heart after God and a heart that God so loved. His heart and God's heart were alike. Having a passion to know the Lord, he walked in tune with Him, which is what the Lord desires for all of us. He wants us to know Him; He wants to reveal Himself to us. Jesus said to give Him a single eye, and the Apostle's response was *"one thing I do."*

This same idea can be gleaned from the story of Mary and Martha in Luke Chapter 10 verses 38-42:

> *"...He [Jesus] entered a certain village; and...Martha welcomed Him into her house. And she had a sister called Mary, who also sat at Jesus' feet and heard His*

word. But Martha was distracted with much serving, and she approached Him and said, Lord, do You not care that my sister has left me to serve alone? Therefore, tell her to help me. And Jesus answered and said to her, 'Martha, Martha, you are worried and troubled about many things; but one thing is needed, and Mary has chosen that good part, which will not be taken away from her.' "

This lesson is applicable to all of us at one time or another, and for many of us, much of the time. These two sisters loved the Lord, having fully demonstrated their faith in Him, their devotion to Him, and a desire to follow Him. Acting as hostess and apparently very eager to please and bless the Lord,

Martha welcomed Jesus into their home. She had labored hard, making the home and meal ready for Him. There was nothing wrong in her wanting to serve and please the Lord. But as she was working in the kitchen, she wasn't able to handle all that she wanted to do, and began to get upset, *"distracted with much serving."* She had taken on a ministry that day for the Lord, but in her inability to handle it, was getting irritated and frustrated. Apparently, she then recalls Mary. Oh, lazy Mary, sitting there in the living room at the feet of Jesus; and here she was, breaking her back for the Lord! From Martha's viewpoint, this wasn't right or fair. Mary ought to be in there helping her.

We can often find ourselves in this same kind of situation. When we are distracted with much serving, before long, we can become irritated with those who are not helping to share the load. Martha's solution was to appeal to the Lord, who was, after all, reasonable and wise, and would certainly take care of this for her. So she asked Him if He cared that Mary had left her breaking her back for Him, and would He tell her to go and help her sister. It is almost presumed that the Lord is going to agree with her and tell Mary to go in and help Martha with the serving. But, Jesus turns to Martha, because the problem was not Mary. The problem was Martha.

In the somewhat humanistic Christianity we have in the church in our day, Martha is often depicted as the hero here and Mary the lazy one. This passage was read one day in the church in which I had come to know the Lord, and about thirty women lined up in front of the congregation. They were given big purple badges to wear, called the Royal Order of Martha. Yes, the Royal Order of Fretting and Being Upset with those who won't help you in your ministry!

But the Lord turned to Martha and gave the powerful revelation that only one thing was necessary. That absolutely shatters the natural mind. Even the dedicated Christian, who reads the Word of God and sees that the Lord says, do this, do that, and do the other, can be thrown off by such an answer. The Lord said only one thing was necessary. Only one thing? Yes, and Mary had chosen that good part, which would not be taken away from her. Mary was sitting at the feet of Jesus

Christ, hearing His word. She was being obedient.

> *"...man shall not live by bread alone, but by every word that proceeds from the mouth of God" (Matthew 4:4).*

She was receiving life itself from the Lord of life, the "good part" which could never be taken away from her.

There are plenty of important things to do in the Christian life. Scripture outlines a number of important things, but there is only one necessary thing. Everything else must take a lower priority in our lives if we are to heed the words of our Lord. As an example to us, both physically and spiritually, Mary was doing the one necessary thing, getting to know her wonderful Lord.

There seems to be a strong implication here not only to guard our quiet time with the Lord, but also that we should never desert the one necessary thing when we start doing the "important" things. We need not only to sit at the feet of the Lord as literally, specifically, and habitually as we can, but also to recognize that we can only abound in the work of the Lord as we remain in that posture in our hearts and minds. The Lord does want us in the kitchen sometimes, but He does not want us in there worried, bothered, distracted, or upset. Even though we may designate a fixed period of time in the morning and evening for abiding in Him, if the rest of the time we are plugging away with all we've got in our own strength, we are going to end up as a Martha, missing out on the very thing the Lord has for us.

The one necessary thing is the receiving of His abundant life through humble dependence upon Him. Years ago the Lord started teaching me on this very issue. I was pastoring at the time, and it was as though He was saying to me, "All right, Pastor Martha, let's look at this again. I appreciate the devotion I see in your heart. You have really wanted to please and serve Me, but it has gone from wanting to please and serve Me to wanting to pound on all those who are letting you down. You're worried and bothered about everything."

The Lord gave me another test on this matter some years ago as I was being sent out to minister in other places, as well as pastoring a local church. Not only was I worried and bothered about things in the local church, but also about the issues that arose in every other place at which I was ministering. Such worries destroy the possibility of really getting to know the Lord, much less making Him known to others. Others see in us just one more harried, worn-out, frustrated, irritated, religious busy-body. Effective ministry can occur only when the Lord has our hearts. We need to be resting at the feet of the Lord Jesus Christ both in our quiet time and in doing the Lord's work, or we will feel like exploding from anxiety. If we consider everything from His perspective, knowing His heart in every circumstance as it arises, looking to Him for His sustaining grace, we will be doing that one "necessary" thing.

"One thing I do." The more I chew on this, the more I recognize that there

is real juice in this heavenly meat. I run out of words to even begin to express the glory I sense is there. It will change priorities, sorting out the necessary, the important, and the urgent. If we lose sight of the "one necessary thing," the urgent can be especially troublesome, because it will go to the top and stampede over the one necessary thing. We are then driven from one deadline to another, rather than being drawn by the leading and guiding of the Lord.

Paul states the "one necessary thing" in another way:

"For to me to live is Christ..." (Philippians 1:21).

Living for Christ results in serving Him and laboring for Him, but it all has to flow out of this reality: To me to live is

Christ. Life in the Lord on this earth is Christ. Getting to know Him, growing in Him, making Him known, abiding in Him and bearing fruit, is Christ.

Early on in my walk with the Lord, I thought I had grown to the place where I could say: "For to me to live is to live for Christ." Such a statement is biblically sound, all right and good. But the Lord has a deeper reality for us to understand. Living our lives for Him and having Him as our very life are two very different things. The difference may be subtle at times, but let us press on to that place where we can say with Paul: *"For to me to live is Christ!"*

If we want to be abounding in the work of the Lord, we need to keep abiding in Him, because abounding without abiding is mere busy activity, which eventually leads to anxiety. As we abide in Him, there is a rest that spills over into our relationships with family, friends, brothers and sisters in Christ, and even the lost. When we look at Jesus as our example, we never see Him in a hurry, though He did so very many things. He was always abiding in the Father:

> *"Do you not believe that I am in the Father, and the Father in Me? The words that I speak to you I do not speak on My own authority; but the Father who dwells in Me does the works"* (John 14:10).

That amazing, glorious, fruitful, perfect life lived out by Jesus here on the earth was the Father living in and through Him. Even though He was the

Son of God, He lived on the earth as the Son of Man, a humble servant.

"As the living Father sent Me, and I live because of the Father, so he who feeds on Me will live because of Me" (John 6:57).

Jesus' priority on the earth was His relationship with the heavenly Father, to know what the Father wanted to do and how He wanted to express His will in and through Him at any given time. Jesus taught that as it was with Him, so it was to be with His followers. As He lived because of the Father, so we will live if we feed on Him. How do we "feed" on the Lord? We do so by trusting in Him, depending on Him, looking to Him, counting on Him. A life so lived becomes like the life of Christ, because we draw on His life. We will be learning how to do this until the day we see Him face to face.

> *"For now we see in a mirror, dimly, but then face to face. Now I know in part, but then I shall know just as I also am known"* (1 Corinthians 13:12).

Until then we need to keep meditating on this truth, allowing His Word to sharpen our priorities. The depth of this simple phrase is unfathomable, but because of this, we can continue to grow in it as we press on to know the Lord.

FORGETTING WHAT LIES BEHIND

The Lord wants us to know that an important aspect of pressing on to do the one necessary thing is forgetting what lies behind:

> *"...forgetting those things which are behind and reaching forward to those things which are ahead" (Philippians 3:13).*

Life in the Lord Jesus Christ is developed in the arena of what lies ahead rather than that which is found by looking back. We need to be thankful for what He did twenty-five years ago, but if the only testimony we have is what He did twenty-five years ago, we have not been growing in knowing the Lord. Praise the Lord for what He did back then; it is not insignificant. It must be followed, however, by that which He does each day thereafter. Those who are all caught up in the things that lie in the past, are not attending to the one necessary thing. Regardless of what happened to you or what kind of family you had, we are called to forget those things.

The Lord does not want us dwelling on past mistakes. Whatever lies behind, the Lord wants us to forget it. Don't dwell on it. There is no life there, and it can easily bring distraction or discouragement. What about something good that happened, something that perhaps we did very well? Dwelling on that will bring pride, and that is the last thing we need! God is opposed to the proud, and we do not want to walk in a place where God is opposed to us.

> *"...God resists the proud, But gives grace to the hum-ble" (James 4:6).*

We should always seek to be in that place of humility where God gives grace. It is the only way that we can move on. We are called to forget what lies behind, no matter how many times others have let us down. If they did so three or three thousand times, it should be treated the same way and it should be forgotten. Some may say this takes all the fun out of life, but the truth is, following such a path is freedom from worry, heartache, and trouble that many of us are just dragging along with us. We are to let it go. We are to lay it down. It will hinder our Christian walk. Holding on to the past does not help in the life in Christ, but makes it impossible to reach forward to what lies ahead.

In a culture that seems to be blind in front with eyes in the back of its head, we are constantly being asked what happened to us before to bring this thing to pass now. Forgetting what lies behind, we are not to allow anything of the past to divert, distract, or hold us back; and it won't, unless we turn our attention in that direction. If we spend any time at all dwelling in the past, most of us will be walking in minefields of mistakes, heartaches, and problems. But if we humbly walk forward with our Lord, forgetting what lies behind, He will cover us with His grace.

Some time ago I dropped in on one of those pop seminars that seem to have captivated the hearts and minds of so many in the church. The sessions were being held right next door to a workshop I was teaching. A handful of people were with me studying the Bible, and next door, approximately 150 people were concentrating on everyone's past. During the question-and-answer period, I asked the brother leading it, who was teaching that you had to get into your past before moving on, "Would you please comment on Philippians 3:12-14, in light of what you are urging us to do?" He grabbed his Bible and started looking for Philippians, and then stopped and asked, "Is this a trick question?"

Is it a trick question to ask a teacher to shine the light of the Word of God on what he is teaching? It is not a trick question; it is an essential question. So he found the passage and said, "Oh yeah, forgetting what's behind...press on. Oh yeah, the reason Paul could do this is because in verses four through six, he had totally dealt with his past." I knew this chapter fairly well, and knew that in it, Paul had said that though there were numerous temptations for him to put confidence in his old life, he counted it all dung. If that is dealing with your past, okay, he dealt with his past.

The point this man was trying to make, however, was that because Paul had fully delved into all of his past, he could press on, which is quite the contrary to what this passage is saying.

Paul said that we are not to put any confidence in our past flesh life, but to count it lost, rubbish, dung, and to press on to know the Lord.

God said that if we would follow Him and are willing to let all of the past lie dead, He would work with us and in us to set us free from our past. If we cannot make ourselves forget those things from the past, we ought to be willing to leave all that behind, and allow God to do the rest.

Our relationship with Jesus Christ is developed in what lies ahead, and there is so much more that lies ahead! If the Lord tarries another day, how much more of Him can we learn this day and tomorrow? If He tarries another week or five or ten years, how much more can we learn and grow in knowing the

Lord? That is the direction into which we need to press, always pressing on to know Him more and more.

Finally we have come to the goal and the prize:

"I press toward the goal for the prize of the upward call of God in Christ Jesus" (Philippians 3:14).

Forgetting what is behind, reaching out, stretching for what God had in their relationship, Paul presses toward the goal of the call that the Lord had for his life. This pressing on is not fleshy, frantic striving, something we are trying to muster up.

"For we...who worship God in the Spirit, rejoice in Christ Jesus,

and have no confidence in the flesh" (Philippians 3:3).

According to Paul, we are to put no confidence in the flesh. Rather it is God at work in us,

"...both to will and to do for His good pleasure" (Philippians 2:13).

We press on toward the goal as God is working in us. What is the goal? The prize includes all the blessings and benefits that come into our lives as we get to know the Lord. Portions of that prize are released into our lives by degree as we grow in knowing Him, as we get closer to that upward call of God in Christ Jesus. It is as though the Father is saying through the apostle, "I'm calling you from heaven; come get to know

My Son." So we press forward with a heavenly gaze, "Lord Jesus, I want to know You!" That is the upward call. In every step of progress, there is a prize. May the Lord stir our hearts to answer that call!

CONCLUSION

We see throughout the Bible that God's desire is to reveal Himself to humanity. He wants His people to get to know Him more and more and for Him to be the highest priority in their lives.

> *"That I may know Him and the power of His resurrection, and the fellowship of His sufferings, being conformed to His death" (Philippians 3:10).*

There is no greater thing in life than knowing the Lord. The Lord wants us to get more acquainted with Him by experiencing the power of His resurrection, through sharing in the fellowship of the suffering He endured here on the earth, and by being conformed to His death as we learn to die to self. Only the Lord could use these means, that seem to counterproductive to the natural mind, to reveal more of His character to those who trust in Him. As we are afflicted, we learn that He is our hope, our strength, our joy, our very life.

The Apostle Paul went through much affliction in His walk with the Lord. He stated that his heart's desire and goal in life was to grow in intimacy with the risen Lord. He wanted to know the Lord so well that his life would be transformed into resurrected living in this spiritually lifeless world. Paul did not want anything to distract him from following after the Lord. He gave no importance to his former life as a religious leader, a Pharisee.

"Brethren, I do not count myself to have apprehended; but one thing I do, forgetting those things which are behind and reaching forward to those things which are ahead" (Philippians 3:13).

Things of the past need not dominate our present. God's grace can cover past failures and pains. Today, we need to look forward to the next work of grace that He wants to bring forth as we continue to humble ourselves before the Lord and fully entrust our lives to Him alone. Essentially, God's heart and desire for His people is to move forward, looking onward and upward.

"I press toward the goal for the prize of the upward call of God in Christ Jesus" (Philippians 3:14).

Ultimately, the goal is to get to know the Lord better. We are to press toward that goal, exerting all of the spiritual strength and energy that God's grace supplies. This is our reply to God's heavenly call to seek Him, to know Him. Along the way, we will partake of the prize that comes with that goal. The prize is every blessing that results from getting to know Him better. Knowing God should be the highest priority in our lives. Day by day in our pilgrimage here on earth, let's press on to know Him more and more!

CLOSING PRAYER

LORD, I ask you to stir my heart to desire this one necessary thing. Enlighten the eyes of my heart. Teach me the depth of it, the extent if it, the application of it, how everything else sorts out in it. May I be one that turns away from the things behind me, and presses on to know You with all my heart, soul, mind and strength. May Your grace be at work abundantly in me. I confcss that if You would leave me to myself, I could not do it. I could not even begin to understand it. I would be in despair and quit. Lord, lead me on! Work in me both to will and to do of Your good pleasure in this great matter of pressing on to know You. I pray these things,

in JESUS' name. Amen.

LICM BOOKS

AVAILABLE IN PAPERBACK AND EBOOK

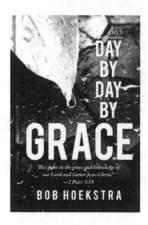

God wants us to know His grace. He wants us to learn about it and experience it in our lives. In these devotionals, Pastor Bob explains that God's grace is much more than forgiveness and new birth. God's grace is much more than sufficient to give us abundant life and much more than what is necessary to change our lives.

Tragically, an increasing number of churches and church leaders are forsaking God's way of counseling and turning to man's ways. They are relying more and more on psychological theories, and less and less on the truth of the Word of God. They are looking to self and others for answers instead of looking to our Wonderful Counselor.

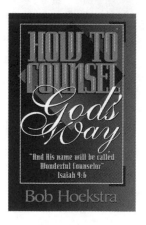

LIVINGINCHRIST.ORG

MEDIA RESOURCES

Knowing God
2 studies

"That I may know Him and the power of His resurrection, and the fellowship of His sufferings, being conformed to His death"
-Philippians 3:10

◄ Growing in knowing the Lord is to be the highest priority in life.

Discipleship Collection
68 studies

"Go therefore and make disciples of all the nations..."
-Matthew 28:19

These studies will encourage, equip, and enable you to know the Lord better and to serve Him fruitfully.

Family God's Way
6 studies

"Unless the Lord builds the house, they labor in vain who build it"
-Psalm 127:1

Families are to be built upon the foundation of a loving relationship with the Lord.

VISIT OUR WEBSITE FOR MORE AVAILABLE RESOURCES

"No more shall every man teach his neighbor, and every man his brother, saying, 'Know the LORD,' for they all shall know Me, from the least of them to the greatest of them, says the LORD..."

- Jeremiah 31:34